S0-BSM-454

# Reporting
# Child Abuse

SCHOOL OF EDUCATION
CURRICULUM LABORATORY
UM-DEARBORN

The Practicing Administrator's Leadership Series
Jerry J. Herman and Janice L. Herman, Editors

**ROADMAPS
TO SUCCESS**

# Other Titles in This Series Include:

**The Path to School Leadership:** A Portable Mentor
Lee G. Bolman and Terrence E. Deal

**Holistic Quality:** Managing, Restructuring, and Empowering Schools
Jerry J. Herman

**Selecting, Managing, and Marketing Technologies**
Jamieson A. McKenzie

**Individuals With Disabilities:** Implementing the Newest Laws
Patricia F. First and Joan L. Curcio

**Violence in the Schools:** How to Proactively Prevent and Defuse It
Joan L. Curcio and Patricia F. First

**Women in Administration:** Facilitators for Change
L. Nan Restine

**Power Learning in the Classroom**
Jamieson A. McKenzie

**Computers: Literacy and Learning**
A Primer for Administrators
George E. Marsh II

**Restructuring Schools:** Doing It Right
Mike M. Milstein

**Dealing With Gangs:** A Handbook for Administrators
Shirley R. Lal, Dhyan Lal, and Charles M. Achilles

**Conflict Resolution:** Building Bridges
Neil Katz and John W. Lawyer

# Reporting Child Abuse

## A Guide to Mandatory Requirements for School Personnel

Karen L. Michaelis

CORWIN PRESS, INC.
A Sage Publications Company
Newbury Park, California

Copyright © 1993 by Corwin Press, Inc.

All rights reserved. No part of this book may be reproduced or utilized in any form or by any means, electronic or mechanical, including photocopying, recording, or by any information storage and retrieval system, without permission in writing from the publisher.

*For information address:*

 Corwin Press, Inc.
A Sage Publications Company
2455 Teller Road
Newbury Park, California 91320

SAGE Publications Ltd.
6 Bonhill Street
London EC2A 4PU
United Kingdom

SAGE Publications India Pvt. Ltd.
M-32 Market
Greater Kailash I
New Delhi 110 048 India

Printed in the United States of America

**Library of Congress Cataloging-in-Publication Data**

Michaelis, Karen L.
  Reporting child abuse : a guide to mandatory requirements for school personnel / Karen. Michaelis.
     p.  cm.
  Includes bibliographical references (p. 60)
  ISBN 0-8039-6100-6 (pb)
  1. Child abuse—Reporting——United States. 2. Abused children—United States—Identification. 3. Teacher-student relationships—United States.  I. Title.
  UV6626.52.M53   1993
  363.2′595554—dc20                                    93-28246

93 94 95 96 10 9 8 7 6 5 4 3 2 1

Sage Production Editor: Marie Louise Penchoen

CL
CI

363.2

# Contents

# Foreword

Karen Michaelis has performed a valuable service for all educators. In *Reporting Child Abuse: A Guide to Mandatory Requirements for School Personnel*, she clearly lays out the responsibilities *all* persons have who work with children—to be on the alert for and report any situation of child abuse.

By compiling the laws and court cases concerning child abuse at the federal level and across all 50 states and the District of Columbia, she has created a mandatory handbook for school personnel and many other professionals. This book catalogues the who, what, and how of reporting suspected and actual child abuse and then goes beyond to consider such related topics as punishment for failure to report, immunity for the reporter, confidentiality, police access to the victims, and the responsibilities of the school district.

Michaelis has organized this book by both specific subject definition and state, so any professional can quickly find the legal requirements relating to a specific position or place of employment. This handbook is a MUST READ reference for all school personnel.

JERRY J. HERMAN
JANICE L. HERMAN
*Series Co-Editors*

# About the Author

**Karen Michaelis** is an Associate Professor at Illinois State University where she teaches school law and is the editor of the *Illinois School Law Quarterly*. She earned her PhD in Educational Administration and JD from the University of Wisconsin, Madison. She is licensed to practice law in the State of Wisconsin and in the Federal District Court for the Western District of Wisconsin and she has experience teaching in Wisconsin public schools at several levels. Her primary teaching interest is school law, but she has taught a variety of educational administration courses, including subjects of the principalship, supervision, organizational leadership, and the politics of education.

One line of Michaelis's research focuses on school administrator's knowledge of the law and how legal information can be made more accessible and useful to public school administrators. An outgrowth of this research, currently being developed, is a desktop reference of school law for administrators, a three-volume practical guide for administrators dealing with student rights, teacher rights, and special education. Other research interests include the development of the student's Fourth Amendment rights, using the adult criminal cases as a basis for comparison, and the evaluation of the federal Indian education policy through the six phases of federal Indian policy.

# Preface

The book is intended to introduce the basic elements necessary to comply with specific state reporting statutes on child abuse. It reflects a compilation and analysis of all 50 states' (plus the District of Columbia) reporting statutes, outlining those requirements imposed on mandatory reporters employed in public schools and in other professions.

In addition to identifying specific requirements by state, I have identified categories common to all state reporting statutes. These categories are used to highlight those areas that school personnel need to consider when reporting suspected child abuse. Each category is discussed and variations within a category are presented. The appendixes at the end of each chapter list both categories and states, showing which states ascribe to various elements within a category and allowing a comparison across states.

Using this organization, a professional can quickly determine what is required within a category, state by state. It is important that all professionals working with children be aware of their legal responsibilities to help keep children from harm.

Because we're dealing with statutory language which is constantly evolving, readers should refer to the actual statute to ensure absolute accuracy.

# Mandatory Reporters: Who Is Required to Report Abuse and Neglect?

State statutes vary greatly in specifying who must report suspected child abuse and neglect. Of the 130 mandatory reporters specified in the 51 child abuse and neglect statutes, two professions predominated. Medical professionals are the most frequently identified mandatory reporters, followed by individuals employed in schools. These two groups of professionals have frequent and prolonged contact with children within the sphere of their professional activities. State legislatures have concluded that members of these professions are more likely than other professions to observe changes in the behavior and health of children in their care. Therefore, medical professionals and educators should be held responsible for reporting suspected instances of child abuse and neglect.

Two other professions, law enforcement officials and members of the clergy, are mentioned less frequently than medical and school professionals but constitute the third and fourth most frequently identified mandatory reporters. Appendix 1-A gives a specific list of mandatory reporters and the states that have labeled them as such.

1

## Appendix 1-A: Mandatory Reporters

1. Any health-related occupation: HI
2. Any other child- or foster-care worker: AR FL IL LA MO NV NH NY ND PA TN WV
3. Any other person called on to render medical assistance to any child: AL ND
4. Any other person having reason to believe: ID IA
5. Any other person having responsibility for care/treatment of children: AZ MA MO
6. Any other person with reasonable cause: DE ID NB NH NJ NM OK TX UT WY
7. Any other person with reasonable cause to know or suspect: RI
8. Any other person who provides child-care services: LA
9. Any other person who provides counseling services to child or family: LA
10. Any person licensed to practice medicine: VA
11. Any professional staff person not previously enumerated: VA
12. Any public or private official: OR
13. Attorney, District/ADA: NY
14. Attorney (unless information is from privileged communication): NV OH WI
15. Audiologist: OH WI
16. Chair of a professional licensing board: ME
17. Child-care center employee or operator: IA
18. Child-care center employer: CO
19. Child-care worker: AK CT HI IL IA KY LA ME MD MN MS OH SC VA WA WI
20. Child, Education advocate assigned to: IL
21. Child health associate: CO
22. Chiropodist: CO
23. Chiropractor: AL AZ CO CT FL HI IL IN KY LA ME MD MA MO MT NV NH NY PA SD TN WI DC
24. Christian Science practitioner: CO IL LA MO MT NV NH NY PA SC VA WV
25. Clergyman: AZ CT LA MN MS MT NV NH ND
26. Clerk/Magistrate of district courts: MA
27. Counselor: AZ IA WI
28. Counselor, Guidance: CT GA ME MD MA

29. Counselor, Licensed professional: OH
30. Counselor, Marriage or Family: LA
31. Counselor, Professional: GA
32. Counselor, School: AR NV NH ND SC SD WA
33. Counselor, Social service: WA
34. Counselor, Substance abuse: CT MA
35. Courts: HI
36. Crisis intervention employees, Paid: AK IL
37. Day-care employees: AL CT ID WA
38. Day care, Licensed/Unlicensed provider: LA
39. Day care, Person paid for caring for children in a day-care center: CT
40. Day-care personnel: ID
41. Day-care workers: AL AR CT FL MA MO MT NH NY ND PA TN DC
42. Dental hygienist: CO IL IA LA ME MD NV NY
43. Dental professional: WV
44. Dentist: AL AZ AR CO CT DE HI IL IN KY LA ME MD MA MS MO MT NV NH NY ND OH OK PA RI SD WI DC
45. Director or staff assistant of nursery school/day-care center: IL IA MT OH WA
46. Doctor/Surgeon: AL AZ AR CO CT DE FL HI ID IL IN KY LA ME MD MA MS MO MT NB NV NH NM NY ND OH OK PA RI SD TN WI DC
47. Domestic violence/sexual assault program, Paid employees: AK IL NV
48. Education professionals: MN
49. Educational administration: MA
50. Employee of public/private facility serving children: FL HI MA NV VA
51. Employers or officers of public/private school: HI
52. Family service work: AR
53. Foster parent: MA
54. Healing arts practitioners: AK DE HI MN VA WA
55. Healing arts, Religious practitioners: ND
56. Health practitioner: IA KY LA MO MT OH SC TN WI
57. Health practitioner, Other: MO
58. Health professional: FL
59. Individual provider of child care: HI
60. Instructor's aide: CA LA
61. Investigator in DA's office: NY

62. Judge: SC TN
63. Law enforcement officials: AL AR CT FL GA HI IL LA ME MD MA MN MO MT NH NM NY ND PA SC SD TN VA WV WI DC
64. Librarian, School: NV
65. Licensed/registered child-care provider: HI IL
66. Medical examiner/Coroner: AL AZ AR CO CT DE FL HI ID IL KY LA ME MD MA MN MO MT NV NH NY ND OH PA RI SD TN WI DC
67. Medical personnel engaged in admission, examination, care, or treatment: AR CO FL IL IA LA MA MO MT NV NH NY PA TN DC
68. Medical professional: WV
69. Mental health professional: AL AR CO CT FL IA IN KY LA ME MD MA MO MT NY ND PA RI SD TN VA WV WI DC
70. Nurses, LPN: AR CO CT GA IL IN LA ME MD NV OH PA SD VA WA DC
71. Nurses, RN: AL AZ CO CT DE FL GA HI ID IL IN KY ME MD MA MS MO MT NB NV NH NM NY ND OH OK PA RI SD TN VA WA WI DC
72. Nurses, School: NH PA WA
73. Nurses, Visiting: NM OH
74. Officers, Administrative officers of institutions: AK
75. Officers, Department of Corrections: AK MA
76. Officers, Juvenile: MO
77. Officers, School: HI
78. Optometrist: AL CO CT HI KY LA MO MT NV NH NY ND PA RI SC WV
79. Organization that provides counseling or treatment re drug/alcohol, Paid employees: AK IL NV ND WI
80. Osteopath: AL AZ AR CO CT DE FL HI IL IN KY ME MD MA MT NH NY OK PA SD TN
81. Parent: AZ
82. Parole officer: HI MA
83. Pathologist: SD
84. Pathologist, Speech: OH
85. Pathologist, Speech/language: WI
86. Peace officers: AL AK AZ AR CO IA KY MO MT NY PA
87. Person rendering spiritual treatment through prayer: OH
88. Person responsible for care of children: MO
89. Pharmacist: AL CO HI WA

90. Podiatrist: AL AZ CO CT HI IL IN LA ME MD MA MO MT NV NY OH PA SD
91. Police officer: CT LA MN
92. Principal: CT LA MS MO
93. Probation officer: HI IL LA MA MO WA
94. Professional licensing board, Chair: MD
95. Psychiatrist: IL LA MA MN NV NH
96. Psychologist: AZ CO CT DE HI IA LA ME MD MA MN MS MO NV NH NY SD WA DC
97. Psychologist, Assistant: IL
98. Psychologist, Certified: IA
99. Psychologist, Intern: GA
100. Psychologist, Licensed: GA OH
101. Psychologist, Licensed school: GA OH
102. Psychologist, Registered: IL
103. Recreational program or facility personnel: ID IL
104. Religious healer: FL MT NV SC SD TN WV
105. School administrators: AK GA MA NV ND PA WA WI
106. School attendance officer: MA
107. School authority: OH
108. School employee: CO DE HI IN MT NB OH
109. School employee, Licensed: IA
110. School, Kindergarten/Nursery: VA
111. School officials: AL AR CO FL ME MD MO MT NH NY SD TN DC
112. School personnel: AZ FL IL IN KY NC TN WV
113. School social workers: GA
114. School staff member: LA
115. Sheriff, County: MN
116. Social services administrator: IL
117. Social services worker: ME MD MA MN NY PA WV DC
118. Social worker: AL AK AZ AR CO CT DE FL GA ID IL IN IA KY LA ME MD MA MS MO MT NB NV NH NM ND OH SC SD TN VA WI
119. Social worker, Clinical: MA
120. Teachers: AL AK AR CA CT DE FL GA ID KY LA ME MD MA MS MO MT NV NH NM ND OH OK PA SC SD TN VA WA WV WI DC
121. Teachers, Visiting: GA
122. Teacher's aide: CA LA
123. Therapist: NH

124. Therapist, Marriage and family: GA NV
125. Therapist, Occupational: WI
126. Therapist, Physical: CO LA WI
127. Therapist, Speech: WI
128. Treatment staff of county department: WI
129. Truant officer: IL
130. Vet: CO
131. Worker in a family care home or child center: CO

# Standard of Proof: How Much Evidence Is Enough?

### When Must a Report Be Filed?

One of the fundamental issues school personnel confront is the question: What does the law require of professional educators in reporting suspected child abuse cases (N.Y. Social Services Law Sec. 413)? Educators in all 50 states, as well as the District of Columbia, are required by state statute to report suspected cases of child abuse "immediately." Typically, child abuse reporting statutes state that "All . . . school teachers and officials shall be required to report or cause a report to be made . . . immediately" (Alabama Code, Sec. 26-14-3[a]). However, very few statutes elaborate on the meaning of the term. One exception is the Alaska reporting statute, which in Sec. 47.17.290(6) states that "immediately" means "as soon as is reasonably possible, and no later than 24 hours."

Other statutes specify that a report must be filed within a specific time limit (Arizona Stat. Annot. Sec. 13-3620 [A]; Connecticut Gen. Stat. Annot., Sec. 17-38a [c]); but most statutes simply require an immediate report without any further indication as to the parameters of the time frame (Colorado Revised Statutes, Sec. 19-3-

304 [1]*; Delaware Stat. Annot., Sec. 904). In the legal context, "immediately" means as soon as there is sufficient evidence from which it is "reasonable" to conclude that a child has been or is being abused.

The question then arises: How much information is necessary to establish sufficient evidence from which it is reasonable to conclude that abuse has occurred? The answer to that question constitutes the standard to which mandatory reporters will be held (see Appendix 1-A). It is not the intent of any of the state legislatures, which have designated school personnel as mandatory reporters, to require educators (or other professionals who work with children) to investigate child abuse cases. However, mandatory reporters are expected to have substantial information (the amount of information varies from state to state) before filing a child abuse report. Currently, 13 states require mandatory reporters to have reasonable "cause to suspect" that child abuse has occurred [1] and 17 states require mandatory reporters to have reasonable "cause to believe" abuse has or will occur [2].

Although the difference between these two standards (reason to suspect and reason to believe) may not at first appear significant, it is, in fact, noteworthy. Originally, the standard in most states was some variation of reason to believe [3]. Recently, several states have changed the standard required of mandatory reporters to that of reason to suspect [4], explaining that less evidence is required to establish a suspicion than to establish belief. Therefore, those states establishing the reason to suspect standard have a lower, more easily satisfied standard than those states still requiring establishment of the reporter's belief that abuse has or will occur (see Appendix 2-A).

Despite the fact that educators are not responsible for formally investigating incidents of suspected child abuse, there is a preliminary investigation that must precede a child abuse report. This initial investigation must be conducted by the mandatory reporter (or the institution in which the child is located and the reporter works) because the report must contain detailed information

---

* Bracketed numbers refer to the listing, found at the end of each chapter, of states affected by the standard or statute being discussed.

about the injuries, the parents' names and whereabouts, as well as other information about the child and his or her family.

During this phase (prior to submitting a child abuse report), the mandatory reporter must understand how much information constitutes sufficient evidence that reasonably leads to the conclusion that a particular child has been abused. This is the point at which the mandatory reporter needs to comprehend the term *reasonable*.

## Reasonableness

The New York reporting statute requires mandatory reporters to file a child abuse report when they have reasonable cause to suspect that a child coming before them in their professional or official capacity is an abused or maltreated child, or when they have reasonable cause to suspect that a child is an abused or maltreated child where the parent, guardian, custodian, or other person legally responsible for such child comes before them in their professional or official capacity and states from personal knowledge facts, conditions or circumstances that, if correct, would render the child an abused or maltreated child (N.Y. Social Services Law Sec. 413).

The term *reasonable* is a favorite in law. It is a word commonly used by lawyers and nonlawyers alike. However, when pressed to articulate a precise definition, those outside (and many within) the legal profession would be hard-pressed to clearly and definitively describe *reasonableness* in terms that overcome the ambiguity inherent in the word. After all, courts have struggled with the definition of *reasonableness* for decades (*Draper v. United States*, 1959; *Ker v. California*, 1963; *Terry v. Ohio*, 1968; *New Jersey v. T.L.O.*, 1985).

*Reasonableness* invariably is defined with reference to the hypothetical reasonable person. The California reporting statute (which served as the model for most state reporting statutes) has defined reasonable suspicion: "For the purposes of this article, 'reasonable suspicion' means that it is objectively reasonable for a person to entertain such a suspicion, based upon facts that could cause a reasonable person in a like position, drawing when appropriate on his or her training and experience, to suspect child abuse" (Cal. Penal Code Sec. 11166 [a] [West, 1991]). (See also Appendix 2-A.)

Thus reasonable suspicion may be established when an educator reviews the facts of a suspicious incident in light of his or her professional training and experience.

## Specific Facts and Circumstances

Any definition of *reasonableness* depends on the individual's ability to "articulate specific facts and circumstances" (*Draper*, above) that support the conclusion that an injury resulted from child abuse. Examples of specific facts and circumstances sufficient to establish the requisite reasonableness include: (a) statements made by the child when questioned by the educator (either teacher or administrator) that would indicate that the injury is not the result of an accident [5]; (b) educator's knowledge of prior unexplained injuries [6]; (c) inconsistencies between the child's version and the parents' version of the origin of the injury [7]; (d) physical signs such as cuts or bruises; and (e) behavioral signs, to name a few (Annotation, 38 Am. Jur. Trials 22) [8].

In other words, educators must take steps to investigate an injury prior to filing a child abuse report. As soon as an educator has articulable facts and circumstances that would lead a reasonable person to conclude that an injury has occurred by other than accidental means, the educator has a duty to "immediately" report the case to the appropriate agency (usually identified in a state's child abuse reporting statute).

The following provides a vivid example of what facts a court will look at to determine if a school official has acted reasonably:

The classroom teacher, perceiving Rochelle's injuries, felt bound to consult the specialized knowledge of the school nurse, and the two, in turn, conferred with the principal. They needed to consider the gravity of the child's hurts, what they knew about her family, and what this portended. Section 51A (Massachusetts child abuse reporting statute) does not require the reporting of every bruise; it requires reporting on the basis of indicators that give reasonable cause to believe that a child is being abused. That conclusion requires an element of judgment to separate an incident from a pattern, the trivial from the serious (*Mattingly v. Casey*, 1987).

As this example illustrates, reasonableness requires some consideration of the surrounding facts and circumstances before an official concludes that abuse has occurred.

### States Affected

1. AK AR CT FL ME MI MS MO NH NJ SD WV WI
2. AZ CT FL GA HI ID IL IN IA KY LA MA NV OR TN TX WA
3. AZ CT FL GA HI ID IL IN IA KY LA MD MA MN NB NV NJ
   OK OR PA SC SD TN TX UT WA WY
4. AK AR CT MI MS MO NH NJ SD WV WI
5. AL AZ CA CO CT FL GA HI IN KY LA MD MA MS MO MT
   NB NV NH NJ NM NY NC OH OK OR TN TX WA DC
6. AL AZ CO CT GA IN LA MD MA MS MO MT NB NV NH
   NJ NM NY OH OK OR PA WA DC
7. LA MD OR
8. AL AZ CA CO CT FL GA HI IN KY LA MD MA MN MS MO
   MT NB NV NH NJ NM NY NC OH OK OR PA WA DC

### Appendix 2-A: Standard

1. Cause to suspect: NC
2. Reason to believe: ID IN IA MD OK PA SC SD UT
3. Reasonable cause/Grounds to believe: AZ CT FL GA HI ID
   IL IN IA KY LA MA NV OR TN TX WA
4. Knows or has reasonable cause to believe: KY MN NB NJ WY
5. Knows or has reasonable cause to suspect: CO MD MT NY
   ND RI TN WY DC
6. Reasonable cause to suspect: AK AR CT FL ME MI MS MO
   NH NJ SD WV WI
7. Reasonable cause to suspect or believe: CT
8. Reasonable suspicion: CA
9. Reporter knows or suspects: AL CO DE MI OH SD

# Protecting the Reporter: What Types of Immunity Exist?

## Purpose of Reporting Statutes

It is important to note that mandatory child abuse reporting statutes have a two-pronged purpose—to increase reporting and to punish for failures to report. Modeled after the California reporting statute (above), virtually all child abuse reporting statutes were enacted to increase the reporting of child abuse for the purpose of decreasing the incidence of child abuse (Besharov, 1986). Thus the theory underlying the purpose of increased reporting is to protect children from further abuse (child abuse is defined as neglect or physical, sexual, psychological or emotional abuse, each of which has its own identifying behavioral characteristics). In addition, many states have identified additional purposes underlying their reporting statutes, including: (a) to preserve or strengthen family life [9], (b) to stabilize the home environment [10], (c) to safeguard and enforce the general welfare of abused and neglected children [11], and (d) to provide a temporary or permanent nurturing and safe environment for children when necessary [12] (see Appendix 3-A).

## Absolute Immunity

To encourage reporting, statutes provide some level of immunity for all professionals who discover evidence of child abuse during the course of the professional contact (see Appendix 3-B). A few states provide absolute immunity for all mandatory reporters [13], but they represent a shrinking minority.

*Absolute immunity* means that regardless of the truth or falsity of the report, no professional required by the reporting statute to report child abuse will be open to legal action, because the underlying purpose of these statutes is to increase the number of reports of child abuse. Initially established in the medical context (*Lehman v. Stephens*, 1986; *Rubinstein v. Baron*, 1987; *Kempster v. Child Protective Services of Department of Social Services*, 1987), absolute immunity was intended to protect mandatory reporters from civil and criminal liability. The purpose of absolute immunity was to ensure that mandatory reporters would be absolutely protected so they would increase their reporting of suspected child abuse, thereby protecting children and reducing the incidence of child abuse. As with most absolute protections, there is the constant fear that a reporter will falsely accuse an individual of child abuse; because of the reporter's absolute protection, the individual would have no recourse for the injury caused by the false accusation. In response to this fear, 43 states and the District of Columbia have provided a mechanism through which aggrieved individuals may seek redress for actual harm resulting from a false report of child abuse [14] (see *Rubenstein v. Baron*, above).

New Jersey's child abuse reporting statute confers absolute privilege where a physician had reasonable cause to suspect child abuse. The physician will not be held liable for defamation even if the physician acted maliciously (*McDonald v. State*, 1985).

## Qualified Immunity

Most states protect mandatory reporters only if child abuse reports are made in good faith (*Thomas v. Beth Israel Hospital, Inc.*,

1989). In those jurisdictions, mandatory reporters have *qualified immunity* [15] (see Appendix 3-B). That is, an accused abuser may seek to hold a reporter civilly liable for damages by attempting to prove that the reporter acted with actual malice [16] or in bad faith [17] in filing the child abuse report.

A teacher and principal were entitled to qualified immunity for reporting suspected child abuse of a student. When questioned about marks on his neck, the student gave two different explanations (cat scratched his neck, mother choked him). Based on Oregon's reporting statute, both the teacher and the principal were entitled to immunity because the report was made in good faith and was based on reasonable suspicion that the child had been abused by his mother (*Miller v. Beck*, 1981). A report by a school psychologist alleging child abuse or maltreatment was challenged by the parents of the suspected victim. Under New York law (N.Y. Social Services Law, Section 419), mandatory reporters are presumed to have acted in good faith in reporting child abuse. As such, they are entitled to immunity from civil liability. To overcome the good faith presumption, the parents would have to prove that the statements made were false and that the school psychologist had acted with actual malice.

A mandatory reporter will not be held liable unless the accused abuser can prove that the statements contained in the report are false and/or that the reporter maliciously filed an abuse report (*Miller v. Beck*, above). However, as the federal district court for the eastern district of Pennsylvania explained in *Roman v. Appleby*, 1983, "good faith . . . must be judged against objective standards rather than alleged motives or allegations of maliciousness."

## Good Faith Reports

The concept of qualified immunity "is based upon the need to ensure principled and conscientious governmental decision-making" (*Crowder v. Lash*, 1982). Traditionally, an official would be entitled to qualified immunity "if the official knew or reasonably should have known that the action he took within the sphere of official responsibility would violate the constitutional rights of [the individual] . . . or if he took the action with malicious intention to cause a constitutional deprivation" (*Wood v. Strickland*, 1975).

However, in 1982, the Supreme Court eliminated the subjective element (malicious intention) from the test. Now, an official is entitled to qualified immunity "so long as official conduct does not violate 'clearly established statutory or constitutional rights of which a reasonable person would have' " (*Roman v. Appleby*, above, at 455, quoting *Harlow v. Fitzgerald*, 1982).

In the context of child abuse reporting statutes, only eight refer to the element of malice [18]. The overwhelming majority of reporting statutes do not require a showing of malice, suggesting that the test for immunity modified in *Harlow* (above) is the norm for most states' qualified immunity statutes.

## Rebuttable Presumption

Child abuse reporting statutes that provide qualified immunity for mandatory reporters are based on the rebuttable presumption that the reporter of suspected child abuse has acted in good faith in making a child abuse report [19] (see Appendix 3-B). The accused abuser has the burden of overcoming the presumption by offering evidence that the reporter did not act in good faith [20]. Only if the presumption is overcome can the accused abuser prevail in an action for damages (*Kempster v. Child Protective Services*, above). But even statutes requiring good faith reporting to establish qualified immunity provide substantial protection for mandatory reporters. "It is all but impossible to rebut the presumption of good faith as long as the person reporting has not been reckless in deciding to report or abusive in dealing with the parents of the child" (Besharov, 1986, p. 71).

## Federal Child Abuse Prevention and Treatment Act

In enacting the Child Abuse Prevention and Treatment Act (42 U.S.C. Sec. 5101), Congress intended to protect mandatory reporters from all claims for damages. The federal statute explicitly calls for states to establish immunity for mandatory reporters against damage suits, including those damage suits brought under 42 U.S.C.S. Sec. 1983 (*Thomas v. Chadwick*, 1990). The federal statute lends additional support for the notion that all mandatory reporters enjoy a high level of protection, even those in jurisdictions that provide the lesser qualified immunity for mandatory reporters. The federal law requires states to "provide for the reporting of known and suspected child abuse and neglect" in order to qualify for federal grants. In so doing, Congress has made the elimination of child abuse official government policy. By attaching strings to the grant of federal money to states, Congress effectively ensured that virtually all states will implement plans for increasing the number of child abuse reports filed by statutorily expanding the class of mandatory reporters while concurrently providing to those reporters immunity from damage suits.

## States Affected

9. AR CT DE GA MI MN MT OR SC TN UT WV WY DC
10. AR CT IA KY OR SC UT WV WY
11. AL GA MI MT NJ OR SC TN WA
12. CT MD MN MT RI
13. AL CA MA NJ
14. AK AZ AR CO CT DE FL GA HI ID IL IN IA KY LA ME MD MI MN MS MO MT NB NV NM NY NC ND OH OK OR PA RI SC SD TN TX UT VA WA WV WY DC
15. AK AZ AR CO CT DE FL GA HI ID IL IN IA KY LA ME MD MI MN MS MO MT NB NV NM NY NC ND OH OK OR PA RI SC SD TN TX UT VA WA WV WY DC
16. AZ ID IN MT NB NM TX VA
17. ID IN MT NM TX VA
18. AZ ID IN MT NB NM TX VA
19. IL IN ME MD MI MS NV NM NY NC ND PA TN WY DC
20. ME MD SC DC

## Appendix 3-A: Purpose

1. Child protection teams publicly discuss agencies' response to reports: CO

2. Compel parent or guardian to perform moral and legal duty owed: MT
3. Cooperate between states: MT
4. Cooperative effort by responsible agency on behalf of children: MD
5. Encourage cooperation among states: AL AR MT SC UT WV
6. Encourage effective reporting: IN
7. Encourage more complete reporting: HI IN IA MT NY ND SC WV
8. Encourage provision of services to protect and treat: ND
9. Establish child protective service to investigate, in each county: IN NY
10. Establish an effective reporting system: SC
11. Establish legal framework to judicially process child abuse cases: ID
12. Fundamental rights, Children have certain fundamental rights which must be protected and preserved: KY
13. Help families overcome problems leading to abuse: DE
14. Identify neglected children: DC
15. Improve parental capacity: OR RI DC
16. Insure thorough and prompt investigation of reports: IA
17. Investigate reports quickly: IN MD
18. Permanent plan for care and custody: ME
19. Preserve family life: AR CT DE GA MI MT OR TN UT WV WY DC
20. Preserve privacy and unity of the family: ID
21. Preserve and strengthen family life: ID MN SC
22. Prevent abuse: LA
23. Prevent further injury/impairment: AR DE FL GA ID NY OR UT WV WY DC
24. Prevent needless delay for permanent placement plans: MD
25. Prevent psychological harm: CA
26. Promote child's welfare and best interest of the state: ID
27. Protect best interest of child: AR CO MD MS UT WY
28. Protect children whose health and well-being may be adversely affected: AK CT ID LA MD MN MT ND SC TN
29. Protect from further abuse: AL CA CO DE FL GA IL IA KY LA ME MD MI MN NJ NY ND OK TN VT WA WV WY DC
30. Protect legal rights of children: NJ
31. Provide for detection and correction through rehabilitation and amelioration: FL

32. Provide in each county an effective child protection service: IN
33. Provide protection: IN
34. Provide protective and counseling services: MN
35. Provide rehab services to child, parent, guardian, custodian: IN IA MD NY
36. Provide temporary or permanent nurturing and safe environment for children when necessary: CT MD MN MT RI
37. Removal from parental custody: ME MD
38. Require reporting in home, school, and community setting: MN
39. Reunify family: ME
40. Right to develop physically, mentally, and emotionally to child's potential: KY
41. Right to educational instruction: KY
42. Right to a secure, stable family: KY
43. Safeguard and enforce the general welfare of abused and neglected children: AL GA MI MT NJ OR SC TN WA
44. Safety, Make home, school, and community safe for children by promoting responsible child care: CT MN
45. Stabilize home environment: AR CT IA KY OR SC UT WV WY
46. Strengthen the family: CT MN SC

### Appendix 3-B: Immunity

- Absolute: AL CA MA NJ
- Qualified: AK AZ AR CO CT DE FL GA HI ID IL IN IA KY LA ME MD MA MI MN MS MO MT NB NV NM NY NC ND OH OK OR PA RI SC SD TN TX UT VA WA WV WY DC
  1. Provided such person is acting in discharge of duties, within scope of their employment: HI NY OH
  2. Exercising due care: OK
  3. Acting in good faith: AR CO CT DE FL GA HI IL IA KY LA ME MD MA MI MN MS NV NY NC ND OH OK OR PA RI SC SD UT WA WV WY DC
  4. Acting in good faith, Is immune from civil liability for invasion of privacy for taking photographs and X-rays: ME
  5. Bad faith: ID IN MT NM TX VA
  6. Bad faith, Prevailing party entitled to attorney fees and costs: OH

7. Good faith presumed: IL IN ME MD MI MS NV NM NY NC ND PA TN WY DC
8. Good faith presumption is rebuttable: ME MD SC DC
9. Good faith, If report was not in good faith, prevailing party gets attorney fees and costs: OH
10. False report, Except intentional: MO
11. With malice: AZ ID IN MT NB NM TX VA

# Penalties: What Is the Cost of Failure to Report or False Reporting?

Many mandatory reporters worry that if they report what they consider to be suspected incidents of child abuse they will be held civilly and/or criminally liable for mistakenly filing child abuse reports that later prove to be unfounded. Although some degree of caution is necessary, the consequences to the child, as well as the reporter, are more severe when the reporter fails to act because of his or her fear of making a mistake.

### Failure to Report

Mandatory child abuse reporting statutes provide a mechanism for punishing those professionals who fail to report suspected child abuse cases (see Appendix 4-A). It is under this point that liability attaches when educators have, within their knowledge, some facts that indicate the possibility that a particular child is being abused but they fail to take action (i.e., does not investigate or report the situation to the social service agency designated by the reporting statute). If a child is later harmed or killed, and information surfaces that an educator was aware of some facts that reasonably could have led to an inference of child abuse, the teacher (as well as the employing district) may be subject to both civil and criminal liability (*Miller v. Beck*, above; *Thomas v. Beth Israel Hospital, Inc.*, above; *Davis v. Durham City Schools*, 1988; *Kempster v. Child Protective Services of Department of Social Services*, above).

Twenty-five reporting statutes contain a failure to report provision that requires proof that the reporter knew from the available information that child abuse had occurred [21]. If the information raises the suspicion that abuse has occurred and the information was known to the reporter, then a failure to file a child abuse report would constitute a knowing failure to report. Liability for failure to report depends on some act or omission by a mandatory reporter that is intended, by the reporter, to purposely prevent a report of abuse from being filed.

## False Reports

Many state reporting statutes contain sections that address a mandatory reporter's failure to report suspected child abuse. Fewer statutes contain sections that address false reports (see Appendix 4-B). However, mandatory reporters also are subject to civil and criminal liability for false reports of child abuse, where the reporter has knowledge of the falsity of the report [22]. Five states require a showing of malice for liability to attach [23] (despite the removal of the malice element at the federal level), and four states reserve liability for false reports that are filed intentionally [24].

It appears that most states consider the risk of false reports of child abuse to be fairly small, judging from the limited number of statutes that address the issue in their reporting statutes. This would seem to indicate that the presumption of good faith in reporting suspected child abuse cases is quite strong and lends support to the conclusion that mandatory reporters have substantial protection from liability, even under qualified immunity.

## States Affected

21. AL AK CA DE FL GA HI IL IN IA LA ME MI MN MT NV NJ NY OK SC SD TN TX WA WV
22. AZ AR CO FL IL IN IA ME MD MI MN OH TN TX WA
23. AZ MI NB TN WA
24. AZ MO TX WA

## Appendix 4-A: Penalties—Failure to Report

1. Civilly liable: IA MI NY
2. Civilly liable, Mandatory reporter who fails or prevents another: MT
3. Intentionally: KY SD
4. Intentionally or knowingly: AZ
5. Knowing(ly): AL AK CA DE FL GA HI IL IN IA LA ME MI MN MT NV NJ NY OK SC SD TN TX WA WV
6. Knowingly and willfully prevents another from reporting: FL
7. Knows or has reason to believe and fails to report: MN
8. Misdemeanor: HI ID IL IN LA MI MN NM NY ND
9. No immunity: MN
10. Purposely: MT
11. Recklessly: AZ
12. Subject to fine: CT MA
13. Willfully: AR CO DE FL GA IL IA LA NV NY ND OK PA UT DC
14. With criminal negligence: AZ

## Appendix 4-B: Penalties—Erroneous (False) Reports

1. Advises another to make false report: FL
2. Disorderly conduct: IL
3. In bad faith: WA
4. Intentionally: AZ MO TX WA
5. Knowingly: AZ AR CO FL IL IN IA ME MD MI MN OH TN TX WA
6. Known to be false: LA NB

7. Liable for civil damages: MN ND
8. Liable for punitive damages: MN
9. Misdemeanor: IN MI
10. Negligently: AR
11. Reckless disregard for truth: LA
12. Recklessly: MN
13. Willfully: AR CO FL IL ND
14. With malice: AZ MI NB TN WA

SCHOOL OF EDUCATION
CURRICULUM LABORATORY
UM-DEARBORN

# Child Abuse Reports:
# What Is Included?

Familiarity with what a state requires a mandatory reporter to include in a child abuse report is essential. Most reporting statutes contain sections that specify: (a) the type of report that must be filed, (b) the content of the report, and (c) the recipient of the report.

## Type of Report

There are two primary methods of filing a child abuse report (see Appendix 5-A). Most statutes explicitly state that a mandatory reporter must report suspected cases of child abuse orally [25]. Further, reports may be made by telephone [26] or FAX [27]. Fourteen states also provide a catch-all category (Otherwise) to cover any conceivable method of verbally reporting child abuse [28].

The second method of filing a child abuse report is most often used as a follow-up to an oral report. Twenty-three states require a written report of suspected child abuse [29]. Five states require a written report only if requested [30]; and 11 states specify the time frame within which the written report must be submitted (within 48 hours [31], within 72 hours [32], within five days 33]). Surprisingly, 8 reporting statutes do not contain any reference to the type of report that must be submitted [34].

## Content of Report

Requirements vary among the states with 51 different items identified by the 50 states and the District of Columbia. However, 9 items emerge as the most frequently required items of information in a child abuse report. The child's name is the most commonly required item of information in reporting statutes [35]. The nature/character and extent of injuries [36] and other pertinent information to establish the cause of injuries [37] tie as the second most frequently required content item (each is contained in 33 state statutes).

Once the child's name and injuries are known, reporting statutes may require such information as: (a) the child's address [38]; (b) names of the child's parents/guardians/caretakers, if known [39]; (c) address(es) of parents [40]; (d) child's age [41]; (e) identity of the abuser [42]. Increasingly, the name of the reporter is requested [43] as well as the reporter's address [44] and any actions taken by the reporting source [45] (see Appendix 5-B).

Finally, mandatory reporters must know to whom the report must be submitted. The most frequently cited recipient was some variation of the Department of Social Services (County or District Department of Social Services, Department of Children and Service, Department of Human Services, to name a few). For the specific name of the social services office mandated to receive abuse reports, the reporting statute should be consulted.

For mandatory reporters working in schools or other child-care facilities and institutions, the report may be made to the person in charge of the facility or the designee [46]. Most statutes containing this provision do not absolve the reporter of responsibility for insuring that a report is actually submitted to the appropriate government agency (social services department or law enforcement agency). The purpose of allowing the head of an institution to submit abuse reports is to reduce the potential for the filing of duplicate reports of the same incident. In a school setting where more than one teacher may suspect that a particular child is being abused, it is appropriate to channel reports through one individual. However, submitting a report to the head of the facility does not necessarily relieve the original reporter of his or her responsibility for reporting the suspected abuse to the state agency. Therefore, if a teacher reports a suspected case of abuse to the building principal, the teacher must follow up with the principal to make sure that the report is actually filed. If, on the follow-up, the teacher discovers that the principal has not reported the case, the teacher then must submit the report to the social service agency or local law enforcement agency.

Once a determination has been made that a child abuse report must be filed, 23 statutes authorize the mandatory reporter to make arrangements for photographs and X rays to be taken of the visible areas of trauma [47] (see Appendix 5-C).

## Recipient of Report

Once sufficient information has been gathered and a school official has decided that a report of child abuse must be filed, then the recipient of the child abuse report must be identified (see Appendix 5-D). The most frequently cited recipient of child abuse reports, cited by almost half of the states, is the person in charge of a facility (i.e., hospital, school, institution, licensed day care) or that person's designee [48].

Only one-fifth of state reporting statutes designate a law enforcement agency [49] as the recipient of child abuse reports, but that number almost doubles when "local police department" [50] is included. Three states identify the "state police" [51] as a recipient of child abuse reports and two states name the "sheriff" as a recipient [52]. Arizona and Ohio have designated "peace officer" as a recipient of abuse reports, and Ohio further describes the peace officer as either a "municipal" or "county" peace officer.

Eight states designate the "department" [53] as a recipient. This category of recipient is usually defined by the state statute and is usually some variation of the department of social services. Eight states have designated the "county or district department of social services" as a recipient of child abuse reports [54]. Although it would seem that the terms *department* and *county or district department of social services* are different labels for the same thing, they are apparently different entities, at least in the state of Colorado. Another variation of the term *department*, used by five states, is the "department of human services" [55].

## States Affected

25. AL CA CO CT DE FL GA HI ID IN IA KY LA MD MA MN
    MS MO NB NV NH NJ NY NC ND OH OK OR PA SC SD TN
    TX VA WA WY DC
26. AL AZ CA CT DE FL GA IA IL KY ME MD MN MS NB NV
    NH NJ NY NC OH OK OR SC SD TN WA WV WI WY
27. NY
28. CT DE FL GA IA KY MN NV NH NJ OR SC SD TN
29. AL AK CA CO CT FL HI IA IN KY LA MA MD MN MS NB
    NH NY ND OH OK PA WY
30. DE GA NH OH WA
31. IA ME MD MA ND WV
32. AZ CT MN
33. LA TX
34. AK AR KS MI MT RI UT VT
35. AL AZ CA CO CT FL GA HI IL IN IA KY LA ME MD MA MN
    MS MO MT NV NH NJ NM NY NC OH OK OR PA TN TX
    WA DC
36. AL AZ CA CO CT FL GA HI IL IN IA KY LA ME MD MA MN
    MS MO MT NB NV NH NJ NM NY NC OH OK OR PA WA DC
37. AL AZ CA CO CT FL GA HI IL IN IA KY LA ME MD MA MS
    MO MT NB NV NH NJ NM NY NC OH OK OR TN TX WA DC
38. AZ CO CT FL GA HI IL IN IA KY LA ME MD MA MS MO
    MT NB NV NH NJ NM NY NC OH OK OR PA TN TX WA DC
39. AL AZ CT FL HI IL IN IA KY LA ME MD MA MI MS MO MT
    NB NV NH NJ NM NY NC OH OK OR PA TN TX WA DC

40. AL AZ CT FL HI IL IN IA KY LA ME MD MA MS MO MT NV NH NJ NM NY NC OH OK OR PA TN TX WA DC
41. AZ CO CT FL GA HI IL IN IA KY LA ME MD MA MS MO MT NB NV NJ NM NY NC OH OK OR PA TN WA DC
42. AL CO FL GA IL IN IA KY LA ME MD MA MN MS MO MT NB NV NH NJ NM NY OK OR PA WA DC
43. CA CO IN IA LA ME MD MA MN MO NY PA DC
44. CO IN IA LA MD MN MO
45. CO IN ME MD MA MO NY PA DC
46. CT GA HI ID IL IN IA KY ME MD MA MS MO NY PA SD TN VA WV WY DC
47. AK AR CA CO FL IL IN IA MD MA MI MT NV NY ND OH OR PA SC SD TN VA WV
48. CT GA HI ID IL IN IA KY ME MD MA MS MO NY PA SD TN VA WV WY DC
49. CO ID IN KY LA MD OR SC UT WA
50. CT NM SD TN WI WY DC
51. CT KY MS
52. MN WI
53. CO IL MD MA ND RI TN WA
54. CO LA MS NM SC SD VA WI
55. IA OH OK WV DC

**Appendix 5-A: Type of Report**

• Oral: AL CA CO CT DE FL GA HI ID IN IA KY LA MD MA MN MS MO NB NV NH NJ NY NC ND OH OK OR PA SC SD TN TX VA WA WY DC

1. Caller gives name, telephone number, and address: NB NC
2. Communication, Direct: AL MD
3. FAX: NY
4. In person: AZ IL OH WI
5. Otherwise: CT DE FL GA IA KY MN NV NH NJ OR SC SD TN
6. Refusal to give name shall not preclude investigation: NC
7. Telephone: AL AZ CA CT DE FL GA IA IL KY ME MD MN MS NB NV NH NJ NY NC OH OK OR SC SD TN WA WV WI WY
8. Within 24 hours: IA ID
9. Within 48 hours: FL TX WA

- Written: AL AZ CA CO CT FL HI IA IN KY LA MA MD MN MS NB NH NY ND OH OK PA WY
  1. By child protection service: IN
  2. Only if requested: DE GA NH OH WA WI DC
  3. Or in writing: NC
  4. Within 48 hours: IA ME MD MA ND WV
  5. Within 72 hours: AZ CT MN
  6. Within 5 days: LA TX
- Law Enforcement Agency
  1. In writing: NM
  2. Name, address, and phone number of reporter: NM
  3. Reports by telephone: NM
  4. Telephone: NM
  5. To a county social services office: NM
- Do not refer to type of report (either oral or written): AK AR KS MI MT RI UT VT

### Appendix 5-B: Content of Report

1. Abuse, Where suspected abuse occurred: PA
2. Abuser, Address of: CO KY MO NV
3. Abuser, Identity of: AL CO FL GA IL IN IA KY LA ME MD MA MN MS MO MT NB NV NH NJ NM NY OK OR PA WA DC
4. Abuser, Relationship to child: NV PA
5. Abusive conduct, Names/addresses of other children threatened by: FL
6. Child, Any other information that would provide assistance to the child: IA
7. Child, Explanation of cause by child, caretaker, other: LA MD OR
8. Child, Address, if not same as parents' or other person's home address: IA
9. Child, Nature and extent of child's dependence on a controlled, dangerous substance: GA OK
10. Child, Removal or keeping: MO
11. Child's address: AZ CO CT FL GA HI IL IN IA KY LA ME MD MA MS MO MT NB NV NH NJ NM NY NC OH OK OR PA TN TX WA DC

12. Child's age: AZ CO CT FL GA HI IL IN IA KY LA ME MD
    MA MS MO MT NB NV NJ NM NY NC OH OK OR PA TN
    WA DC
13. Child's name: AL AZ CA CO CT FL GA HI IL IN IA KY LA
    ME MD MA MN MS MO MT NV NH NJ NM NY NC OH OK
    OR PA TN TX WA DC
14. Child's parents, Name, age, and sex: DC
15. Child's race: CO LA MS MO NY
16. Child's sex: CO IN LA ME MD MA MS MO NV NY PA DC
17. Child's siblings, Name, age, and sex: DC
18. Child's whereabouts: AL CA ME MD NC
19. Children, Name, age, and condition of other children in same
    home: IA
20. Coroner, Notifying coroner or medical examiner: MO
21. Custody, Name and address of person having custody (if not
    parent or guardian): MN
22. Developmentally disabled person's name and address: VA
23. Developmentally disabled person's age: VA
24. Family, Composition: CO LA ME MD MO NY PA
25. Incident, Information relevant to: CA MN TN
26. Information, Any other information required by the depart-
    ment: IN MA PA
27. Information, Other pertinent information to establish cause
    of injuries: AL AZ CA CO CT FL GA HI IL IN IA KY LA ME
    MD MA MS MO MT NB NV NH NJ NM NY NC OH OK OR
    TN TX WA DC
28. Injuries, Description: ME MD
29. Injuries, Explanation: ME
30. Injuries, Evidence of previous: AL AZ CO CT GA IL IN IA LA
    ME MD MA MS MO MT NB NV NH NJ NM NY OH OK OR
    PA WA DC
31. Injuries, Evidence of child and siblings: IN ME MD
32. Injuries, Nature/character and extent: AL AZ CA CO CT FL
    GA HI IL IN IA KY LA ME MD MA MN MS MO MT NB NV
    NH NJ NM NY NC OH OK OR PA WA DC
33. Neglect, Nature and extent: VA
34. Neglect, Nature, extent, and cause: LA
35. Parents/guardians/caretaker, Address: AL AZ CT FL HI IL
    IN IA KY LA ME MD MA MS MO MT NV NH NJ NM NY
    NC OH OK OR PA TN TX WA DC

36. Parents/guardians/caretaker, Names: AL AZ CT FL HI IL IN IA KY LA ME MD MA MI MS MO MT NB NV NH NJ NM NY NC OH OK OR PA TN TX WA DC
37. Photos and X rays of child's injuries: GA IN MD MO
38. Report, Source: CO IN ME MD MO NY PA
39. Reporter, Address: CO IN IA LA MD MN MO
40. Reporter, Any action taken by reporting source: CO IN ME MD MA MO NY PA DC
41. Reporter, Notifying coroner: IN
42. Reporter, Removal or keeping child: IN
43. Reporter, Taking photos or X rays: IN
44. Reporter, Any other information reporter believes is relevant: LA ME MD
45. Reporter, Where reporter can be reached: IN ME MD MN MO NY PA DC
46. Reporter's account of how child came to attention: LA MA MT VA
47. Reporter's name: CA CO IN IA LA ME MD MA MN MO NY PA DC
48. Reporter's occupation: ME MD MO DC
49. Residential facility, Name and address where child resides: NY
50. Sexual abuse, Including description of photos and X-rays: ME
51. Sexual abuse, Nature and extent: VA

## Appendix 5-C: Photographs and X Rays

- Photographs and X-rays: AK AR CA CO FL IL IN IA MD MA MI MT NV NY ND OH OR PA SC SD TN VA WV
- Photographs: ME
- Videotape: TN

## Appendix 5-D: Recipient of Report

1. Attorney, State's: SD
2. Cabinet or designated representative: KY
3. Central register: IL
4. Child protection services: IN LA WY

5. Child, Protective services of Department of Economic Security: AZ
6. Children, Department of Children and Services: IL OR
7. Children Services Board: OH
8. Commonwealth's or county attorney: KY
9. Department: CO IL MD MA ND RI TN WA
10. Department, Central abuse registry and tracking system: FL
11. Facility, Person in charge/delegate of: CT GA HI ID IL IN IA KY ME MD MA MS MO NY PA SD TN VA WV WY DC
12. Family, Department of Family Services: MT
13. Health, Department of Health & Rehabilitative Services: FL
14. Health, Department of Health & Welfare: ID
15. Human Services, Department of: IA OH OK WV DC
16. Judge, Having juvenile jurisdiction: TN
17. Law enforcement agency: CO ID IN KY LA MD OR SC UT WA
18. Peace officer: AZ
19. Peace officer, Municipal or county: OH
20. Police department, Local: CT NM SD TN WI WY DC
21. Police, State: CT KY MS
22. Sheriff: MN WI
23. Social services, County or district department: CO LA MS NM SC SD VA WI
24. Social Services, Director of: NC
25. State Commissioner of Children and Youth, or representative: CT
26. Tribal government (for American Indian children): WI
27. Welfare, Local agency: MN
28. Youth, Division of youth and family services: NJ

# Definitions: How Do They Vary?

There is an amazing variety in the terms defined in state child abuse reporting statutes. A review of the 51 reporting statutes (including the District of Columbia) revealed definitions of 240 distinct terms (see Appendix 6-A). There is some overlap in eight categories, and for these the specific variations have been noted.

For instance, 32 states provide a definition for the term *abuse* [56] (see definitions 3-9 in Appendix 6-A). Georgia, Idaho, and Washington, DC have not been included in this category because they have defined the term as "abused" rather than "abuse." Some states combine the terms "abuse or neglect" in one definition [57]. Variations within that category include "abuse or neglect of a child" (Nevada, sec. 432 B.020), "abuse and neglect" (Oklahoma, sec. 845), and "abused or neglected child" (South Carolina, sec. 20-7-490). "Abuse in out-of-home care" (California), "institutional abuse" (Colorado), "intrafamilial abuse" (Colorado), "physical abuse" (Minnesota), and "third-party abuse" (Colorado) are other variations that appear in some child abuse reporting statutes.

Many of the terms defined appear in only one state's reporting statute. There are no terms that are defined by all states. There are, however, a few terms that appear in the definition section of several state statutes. Thirty-two states [58] have defined *child*. Other states have added qualifiers, such as *child abuse* [59]. Delaware and Utah have provided a definition for "child abuse and neglect," and six states have defined "child abuse or neglect" [60]. Five statutes include a definition of an *abused child* [61], and six statutes contain a definition of an *abused or neglected child* [62]. Rhode Island has included a slightly different term in its definition section—"abused and/or neglected child."

The *child* category includes several additional variations within a number of individual state child abuse reporting statutes. Two variations exist for the terms *child neglect* [63] and *neglected child* [64]. The remaining variations within the *child* category generally refer to child protection agencies (see Appendix 6-A, definitions 34-42).

Of the remaining definitions, only 12 appear in at least 6 reporting statutes. For example, seven statutes included a definition of *court* [65]. The most commonly defined term, *department*, appears in 19 reporting statutes [66], followed closely by *sexual abuse,* which appears in 15 reporting statutes [67]. *Mental injury* is defined in 13 statutes [68] and 12 states have defined *person responsible for child's welfare* [69]. Two terms, *physical injury* [70] and *sexual exploitation* [71], were defined by 10 states. Of those 10 states, 3 states defined both terms (Montana, Nevada, and Oregon).

There are 12 variations of the term *report*. Most of the variations are contained in three or fewer state reporting statutes. One term, *unfounded report,* however, appears in nine statutes [72]. The term *law enforcement agency* is defined in eight reporting statutes [73], *custodian* is defined in nine reporting statutes [74], and *institutional child care or neglect* [75] and *parent* [76] are defined in six reporting statutes.

The most notable thing about the compilation of the terms defined by each state reporting statute is that, contrary to what was expected, each state has independently developed, in greater or lesser detail, a list of terms that is unique to each particular state. There is less overlap of terms between states than one might expect. But, frequently, terms included in the definition section of one state's reporting statute are incorporated and ultimately defined in a section other than the definition section in another state.

## States Affected

56. AL AK AZ AR CO DE FL HI IL IN IA LA ME MD MI MN MO MT NB NV NJ NY ND OK OR RI SC TX UT WA WI WY
57. ME NB NV OK SC
58. AL AK AZ AR CA CT FL GA ID IL IA LA ME MD MI MO MT NV NH NM ND OH OK OR RI SC UT VT VA WA WI WY
59. CA GA IA MI NJ PA
60. AK FL HI IN SD WA
61. IL NH NJ NM ND
62. FL MT RI SC VT VA
63. MI
64. ID IL NH NM ND
65. MD NV NH NM OH (juvenile court) VA WA
66. AK AR CO FL HI ID IL IN IA MD (local department) MI MT NB ND PA RI TN VA WA
67. AR CA (of child) LA MD MI MN MT NV NH OK OR PA TN UT VT
68. AK FL ID MN MT NV OR RI SC TN TX VT WY
69. AK AR (legally responsible) IL MT NV NH ND RI SC TN (other person responsible) VT WY
70. AZ FL MT NV OR SC TX VT WI WY
71. AK AR GA MI MT NV OK OR UT WA
72. AR CO FL IL NH PA SC UT WY
73. CO (local) ID IL MD NB RI WA DC
74. ID ME MD NV NH NJ NM NY OH
75. FL NH ND RI (abuse and neglect) SC (abuse and neglect) WY
76. CT ME NV NH NJ NM

### Appendix 6-A: Definitions

1. Abandoned: ID NH
2. Abandonment: ME NJ
3. Abuse: AL AK AZ AR CO DE FL HI IN IA LA ME MD MI MO MT NB NV NJ NY ND OK OR RI SC TX UT WA WI WY
4. Abuse in out-of-home care: CA CO FL
5. Abuse, Institutional: CO
6. Abuse, Intrafamilial: CO

7. Abuse or neglect: ME NB NV (of a child) OK (A and N) SC (abused or neglected child)
8. Abuse, Physical: MN
9. Abuse, Third-party: CO
10. Abused: DC GA ID
11. Adjudicatory hearing: ID NH
12. Administration: MD
13. Adult: NM OH
14. Agency, Authorized: ID
15. Agency that provides protective services: NV
16. Agreement for temporary custody: OH
17. Assessment: MN
18. Bureau: NH
19. Caretaker: AR LA
20. Case permanency plan: KY
21. Case progress report: KY
22. Case record: KY
23. Child: AL AK AZ AR CA CT FL GA ID IL IA LA ME MD MI MO MT NV NH NM ND OH OK OR RI SC UT VT VA WA WI WY
24. Child abuse: CA GA IA MI NJ PA
25. Child abuse and neglect: DE UT
26. Child abuse or neglect: AK FL HI IN SD WA
27. Child, Abused: IL NH NJ NM ND
28. Child, Abused or neglected: FL MT RI (and/or) SC VT VA
29. Child advocate coordinator: ID
30. Child, Delinquent: NM
31. Child in need of supervision: NM SD
32. Child neglect: MI
33. Child, Neglected: ID IL NH NM ND
34. Child placing agency: ID NH OH (private)
35. Child protection proceeding: ME
36. Child protection register: DC
37. Child protection team: CO FL MT ND (local)
38. Child protective agency: CA WY
39. Child protective investigation: SC
40. Child protective investigator: RI
41. Child protective service: IL (unit) PA WA
42. Child protective services section: WA
43. Child, Removal of: Md
44. Child welfare agency: TN

45. Child welfare services ombudsman: ME
46. Child-care agency: CT NH
47. Child-care custodian: CA
48. Child-care pornography: LA
49. Child-care provider: AK
50. Child-care services: PA
51. Child day-care center: OH
52. Child day-care provider: OH
53. Clergy: WA
54. Commissioner: MN
55. Commit: ID OH
56. Committee: NV
57. Complaint: VA
58. Confidential access to a child: IA
59. Confirmed: CO
60. Consent order: NH
61. Cooperation with an investigation: PA
62. Corporal punishment or injury: CA
63. Council: UT
64. Counsellor, Licensed professional: OH
65. County department: CO
66. County director: CO
67. Court: MD NV NH NM OH (juvenile court) VA WA
68. Court proceedings: WY
69. Criminal negligence: AK
70. Cruelty: NJ
71. Cruelty, Willful or unjustifiable punishment of a child: CA
72. Custodian: ID ME MD NV NH NJ NM NY OH
73. Danger, Imminent: NH WY
74. Delinquent act: NM
75. Department: AK AR CO FL HI ID IL IN IA MD (local department) MI MT NB ND PA RI TN VA WA
76. Dependent youth: MT
77. Detention: OH
78. Detention facility: NM
79. Director: IN MO
80. Disposition hearing: ID NH (dispositional hearing)
81. Division: IN MO NV (welfare) NH
82. Duly constituted authority: AL
83. Educator or human service worker: MD
84. Emotional damage: WI

85. Evidence, Credible: DC
86. Evidence, Relevant: MI
87. Expunge: MI PA
88. Facility: MN
89. Family members: PA
90. Family or household member: ID MD (family member)
91. Foster care: KY
92. Foster care, Approved: OH
93. Foster home: NH OH
94. Foster home, Certified: OH
95. Grant administrator: ID
96. Guardian: NH NM OH
97. Guardian ad litem: ID TN DC
98. Guardian, Program: ID
99. Guardianship: NM
100. Harm: FL ND
101. Harm or threatened harm: UT
102. Harm, Serious: ME
103. Harm threatened to a child: OR SC (threatened harm) VT (threatened harm)
104. Harm threatened to a child's health or welfare: MT
105. Harm to a child's health or welfare: MT SC TN VT
106. Health care provider: IN MD
107. Health practitioner: IA LA MD
108. Household: MD
109. Household member: MD
110. Immediately: AK MN
111. Incest: UT
112. Indian child: WI
113. Injury, Nonaccidental: IA
114. Injury, Serious: ME
115. Injury, Threatened: MN
116. Institution: AK RI WA
117. Institutional child abuse or neglect: FL NH ND RI (A and N) SC (A and N) WY
118. Institutional child sexual abuse: TN
119. Investigation, Under: PA
120. Jeopardy to health or welfare: ME
121. Judge: NM OH (juvenile judge)
122. Law enforcement agency: CO (local) ID IL MD NB RI WA DC
123. Legal custody: ID NH NM OH
124. Legal supervision: NH

125. Licensed mental health professional: ME
126. Licensed or unlicensed child-care organization: MI
127. Limited emancipation: MT
128. Local child protective service agency: SC
129. Local citizen review board: KY
130. Local department: VA
131. Local office file: MI
132. Local state's attorney: MD
133. Malice: WA
134. Maltreatment: AK
135. Mandatory reporter: LA
136. Medical practitioner: CA
137. Mental health practitioner: IA
138. Mental health professional: IA
139. Mental health social services practitioner: LA
140. Mental illness: OH
141. Mental injury: AK FL ID MN MT NV OR RI SC TN TX VT WY
142. Mentally retarded person: OH
143. Molestation: UT
144. Multidisciplinary team: VT
145. Neglect: AL AK AR CA CO DE FL GA HI ID (neglected) IL
     IN LA ME MD MI (child) MN MO MT NB NJ ND NV OK RI
     SC TX UT WA WI WY
146. Neglect, General: CA
147. Neglect, Severe: CA
148. Negligent treatment or maltreatment: NV OR
149. Nonmedical practitioner: CA
150. Notice: NH
151. Operator: MN
152. Organization: AK OH
153. Out-of-home care: OH
154. Out-of-home child abuse: OH
155. Out-of-home child care neglect: OH
156. Parent: CT ME NV NH NJ NM
157. Parent, Custodial: ME
158. Parent or guardian: NJ
159. Parental care, Adequate: OH
160. Permanence: KY
161. Permanent custody: OH
162. Permanent plan: ME
163. Permanent surrender: OH
164. Perpetrator: IL

165. Person: LA ME NM
166. Person, Other responsible for the child's welfare: FL
167. Person responsible: AL AK CO CT IA FL IL LA ME MD MI MN MO MT NV ND RI SC UT WY
168. Person responsible for child's care, custody, or welfare: TX
169. Person responsible for child's care in out-of-home care: OH
170. Person responsible for child's welfare: AK AR (legally responsible) IL MT NV NH ND RI SC TN (other) VT WY
171. Person responsible for the care of a child: IA MN (child's care) UT (child's care)
172. Person responsible for the child: ME
173. Person responsible for the health, welfare, or care of child/youth: CT MI (health or welfare)
174. Pharmacist: WA
175. Physical injury: AZ FL MN MT NV OR SC TX VT WI WY
176. Physical injury, Serious: AZ
177. Physical or mental injury, Inflicts or allows to be inflicted upon the child: FL
178. Physician: FL RI
179. Police: DC
180. Police officer: MD
181. Practice of social services: MN
182. Practitioner of the healing arts: AK WA
183. Preventive services: KY
184. Probable cause: NH RI SC
185. Probation: OH
186. Professional school personnel: WA
187. Protective custody: NH
188. Protective custody, Temporary: IL OH (temporary custody)
189. Protective order: ID
190. Protective services: ND SC (protective services unit)
191. Protective supervision: CT ID NH OH
192. Psychiatrist: OH
193. Psychologist: OH WA
194. Public or private official: OR
195. Reason to believe: IN
196. Reasonable cause to suspect: AK
197. Reasonable efforts: KY
198. Reasonable suspicion/Cause to suspect: AK IN
199. Record: WI
200. Registry: IA
201. Registry, Central: MI

202. Report: HI MN VA DC
203. Report, An undetermined: IL
204. Report, Confirmed: CO FL
205. Report, Founded: NH PA
206. Report, Indicated: IL PA SC
207. Report, Proposed confirmed: FL
208. Report, Subject of the: IL PA SC UT WY
209. Report, Substantiated: VT
210. Report, Supported: DC
211. Report, Suspected: SC
212. Report, Unfounded: AR CO FL IL NH PA SC UT WY
213. Report, Unsupported: DC
214. Reporter: WI
215. Residual parental rights and responsibilities: ID NH OH (privileges)
216. Responsible for the care, custody, and control of the child (those): MT
217. Restitution: NM
218. Reunification services: KY
219. Risk, Substantial: WY
220. School district: AK
221. Secretary: PA
222. Sexual abuse: AR CA (of child) LA MD MI MN MT NV NH OK OR PA TN UT VT
223. Sexual activity: AR OH
224. Sexual assault: CA
225. Sexual exploitation: AK AR GA MI MT NV OK OR UT WA
226. Sexual intercourse or sexual contact: WI
227. Shelter care: ID OH (shelter)
228. Social service counselor: WA
229. Social worker: MT OH OR (licensed clinical)
230. State agency: WY
231. State board: CO
232. State child protection team: ND
233. State citizen review board: KY
234. State department: CO
235. Subject: UT WI
236. Tribal agent: WI
237. Tribunal: NM
238. Victim of child abuse or neglect: IN
239. Withholding of medically indicated treatment: MT
240. Youth in need of care: MT

# Child Abuse Training: What Are the State Requirements?

Twelve states have child abuse training provisions for mandatory reporters [77]. As with most child abuse statutes, there is wide variety and little consistency across state statutes regarding the elements to be included in child abuse training programs (see Appendix 7-A). Iowa is the only state that specifies that mandatory reporters must have additional training every five years after an initial two hours of training. Oregon provides training in the assessment of the risk of child abuse, and Florida, Iowa, and New York include in their training programs the diagnosis and cause of child abuse.

The elements of child abuse training programs are spelled out with some specificity. Iowa and South Carolina alert mandatory reporters to the duties of individual reporters and the agencies employing mandatory reporters. Five states require mandatory reporters to learn how to identify child abuse [78]. In addition to identifying child abuse, Iowa's training statute also included information on reporting child abuse.

Some child abuse training statutes focus on powers [79], obligations [80], and responsibilities [81] of mandatory reporters of the employing agencies. Other statutes provide for instruction in child abuse reporting laws [82], the prevention of child abuse [83], the role of the mandatory reporter (Arkansas), interview techniques (Oregon), and investigation techniques (Arkansas, Oregon).

## States Affected

77. AK CA FL HI IL IA NY OH OR SC WV WI
78. CA HI OR WV WI
79. FL IA NY
80. FL IA NY
81. FL IA NY SC
82. AK CA
83. OH WI

## Appendix 7-A: Child Abuse Training

- Child Abuse Training: AK CA FL HI IL IA NY OH OR SC WV WI
  1. Additional training every five years: IA
  2. Agencies and organizations: AK
  3. Assess risk to child: OR
  4. Diagnosis and cause of child abuse: FL IA NY
  5. Duties of person/agency: IA SC
  6. Identification, Child abuse: CA HI IA OR WV WI
  7. Identification and reporting: IA
  8. Laws: AK CA
  9. Nature of problem/Extent of child abuse: SC
  10. Obligations of person/agency: FL IA NY
  11. Powers of person/agency: FL IA NY
  12. Prevention of child abuse: OH WI
  13. Procedures: AK FL NY
  14. Reporting/Requirements: CA IL IA NY
  15. Responsibilities of person/agency: FL IA NY SC
  16. Role of mandatory reporter: AK
  17. Techniques: AK
  18. Techniques, Interview: OR
  19. Techniques, Investigation: AK OR
  20. Treatment, Child abuse: WV WI
  21. Two hours of training: IA

# Confidentiality: How Are Reports and Privileged Communications Protected?

Thirty states explicitly provide for confidentiality [84] of the information contained in a child abuse report (see Appendix 8-A). Only seven states have a provision that keeps confidential the identity of the reporter [85], and Florida is the only state that does not allow the identity of the reporter to be released without the consent of the reporter. The conclusion that emerges from a review of confidentiality provisions is that slightly more than half of the states protect the information contained in the child abuse report from disclosure, but there is significantly less concern for the release of the reporter's identity.

Statutes vary greatly with regard to the types of relationships entitled to privilege (relatively few) and those that, in the context of child abuse, enjoy no privilege (see Appendix 8-B). Three types of relationships that enjoy privileged status in other legal contexts frequently are not privileged when they arise in the context of child abuse. Some exceptions are husband/wife, physician/patient, clergy/penitent.

The husband/wife relationship [86] is not privileged when a spouse knows that his or her child is being abused by the other spouse. In fact, failure of one spouse to report child abuse inflicted by the other spouse may result in criminal liability for both spouses, not just the perpetrator. Moreover, the usual physician/patient privilege does not extend to communications to a physician in the course of a professional consultation [87] nor to a professional person who receives information of child abuse from a person confessing that the abuse was inflicted by that person [88].

The message is quite clear—child abuse is a pervasive problem today that requires extreme measures to insure that perpetrators of child abuse will not be protected by a privileged communication. The underlying policy behind the abrogation of traditional privileges is that society has a responsibility toward children to keep them from harm.

One privileged relationship, however, is recognized despite the social policy of eliminating child abuse by encouraging child abuse reporting by professionals. Twenty-one statutes explicitly recognize the attorney/client privilege, even when a client confesses to having abused a child. The obvious reason for continued recognition of the attorney/client privilege in the child abuse context is to insure that even an individual accused of child abuse will have access to legal representation. The existence of the attorney/client privilege is most likely implied in the 29 states that have not explicitly included that privilege in the reporting statute.

## States Affected

84. AK CA FL HI IL IN KY ME MD MA MI MN MO MT NB NH NJ ND OH OK OR PA SC SD TN TX UT WV WI WY
85. FL HI MI MO OH TN TX
86. AR CO FL HI ID IN IA KY ME MD MI NB NC ND OR SC TN VA WV WY DC
87. AZ CO HI ID ME MS MD MT NB NC OK OR VA WY DC
88. AZ AR CO FL IL KY ND SC WV

## Appendix 8-A: Confidentiality

- Confidentiality: AK CA FL HI IL IN KY ME MD MA MI MN MO MT NB NH NJ ND OH OK OR PA SC SD TN TX UT WV WI WY
  1. Identity of reporter: FL HI MI MO OH TN TX
  2. Identity of reporter cannot be released without consent of reporter: FL
  3. Name of person: OH TN

## Appendix 8-B: Privilege

- No privilege for
  1. Counselor: ID
  2. Day-care center workers: ID
  3. Educator: MD
  4. Health care provider/patient: IN IA
  5. Health practitioner: IA
  6. Human services worker: MD
  7. Husband/wife: AR CO FL HI ID IN IA KY ME MD MI NB NC ND OR SC TN VA WV WY DC
  8. Interpreter of handicapped person: MS
  9. Mental health professional: IA
  10. Minister, Including Christian Science Practitioner: AR ID RI UT
  11. No one has privilege except attorney/client: IL LA OK PA WY
  12. Nurses: OR
  13. Patient/registered professional nurse: CO
  14. Physician/patient: AZ CO HI ID ME MS MD MT NB NC OK OR VA WY DC
  15. Police officer: MD
  16. Professional person/person confessing: AZ AR CO FL IL KY ND SC WV
  17. Psychiatrist/patient: TN
  18. Psychologist/client: HI MS NC TN WY
  19. Psychotherapist/patient: ME MD OR
  20. School, Certified psychologist/client: CO
  21. School counselor/student: IN
  22. School professional: ID
  23. School staff members: OR
  24. Social workers (registered clinical): OR

- Privilege exists for
  1. Attorney/client: AZ AR DE FL ID KY LA MA MI MO MT NV NM ND OH OR SC SD TN TX WV
  2. Clergy: AZ MI OR UT
  3. Clergy, Including Christian Science Practitioner: LA
  4. Clergy/penitent: KY LA MT SC
  5. Physician/patient: OH
  6. Psychiatrist: OR
  7. Psychologist: OR
  8. School counselor: NC

# Police Investigations: What Guides Access to the Victim?

## Access to Victim on School Property

A new category is emerging in a handful of states that specifies the circumstances under which school personnel may be required to allow law enforcement officials to have access, on school property, to the victim of child abuse [89] (see Appendix 9-A).

Wyoming and Minnesota have provided some details to add meaning to exactly what "access to a victim" could entail. In Wyoming, which school personnel may attend an interview on school property is quite specifically delineated. Minnesota has provided a more general framework, beginning with the provision that an interview at the school is to occur within 24 hours after school officials have been notified that law enforcement officials intend to conduct such an interview (unless school officials and welfare or law enforcement agencies agree to an alternative time). In addition, it is the law enforcement official who has the authority to determine who may attend the interview. Although law enforcement officials control the interview, the Minnesota statute provides that school officials may determine the time, place, and manner of the interview on school property.

## States Affected

89. CA, MN, NM, ND, WY

## Appendix 9-A: Access to the Victim

- Access to the Victim: CA MN NM ND WY
  1. Interview at school shall occur within 24 hours after notification: MN
  2. Law enforcement official determines who may attend: MN
  3. Person who can attend an interview on school property: WY
     a. Principal: WY
     b. Designee: WY
     c. Teacher: WY
     d. Counselor: WY
     e. Specialist employed by school district who monitors child abuse cases: WY
  4. School administration or staff member cannot reveal any information from investigation: OR
  5. School official, unless school official is perpetrator: MN
  6. Time, place, or manner of interview is at discretion of school officials: MN
  7. Unless school officials and welfare or law enforcement agency agree to an alternative time: MN
  8. Without consent or presence of school personnel: VA

SCHOOL OF EDUCATION
CURRICULUM LABORATORY
UM-DEARBORN

# Child Abuse in Public Schools: What Are the District's Responsibilities?

## School Employees as Perpetrators

Colorado and Connecticut are the only two states that specifically address the issue of school employees as perpetrators of child abuse (see Appendix 10-A). The Connecticut statute is, by far, the more comprehensive of the two statutes.

In Connecticut, a school employee is required to report suspected child abuse inflicted by another school employee. The report must be made to the superintendent of the school district. On receipt of the report, the superintendent is required to "immediately notify the child's parents or other person responsible for the child's care" (Conn. Gen. Stats. Sec. 17a-101 [b]). The superintendent is then required to report orally or cause a report to be made to the State Commissioner of Children and Youth Services (or his or her representative), the local police department, or the state police. The oral report is to be followed within 72 hours by a written report to one of the above-mentioned agencies (Conn. Gen. Stat. Sec. 17a-101 [c]).

In addition, when the investigation of child abuse indicates that the abuse has been inflicted by a "certified public school employee" (Conn. Gen. Stat. Sec. 17a-101 [e][1]), that individual may be suspended with pay by the superintendent. The superintendent, however, may not diminish or terminate the employee's benefits (Conn. Gen. Stat. Sec. 17a-101 [e]). Further, the superintendent must specify the "reasons for and conditions of the suspension" (Conn. Gen. Stat. Sec. 17a-101 [e][1]). The employee's suspension may be changed only by the Board of Education through the provisions of Sec. 10-151 (Conn. Gen. Stat. Sec. 17a-101 [e] [1]).

When a school employee has been convicted of a crime of child abuse, the state's attorney is required to notify the superintendent of the employing district as well as the state board of education of the conviction. After such notification, the state board of education is authorized to begin certification revocation proceedings under Sec. 10-145a (Conn. Gen. Stat. Sec. 17a-101 [f] [3]).

In Colorado, the reporting statute provides two remedial measures where "a teacher, employee, volunteer or staff person of an institution" is suspected of abusing a child (Colo. Rev. Stat. Sec. 19-3-308 [4] [c]). The suspected abuser may be temporarily suspended with pay or reassigned to alternative duties that would remove the abuser from contact with children. These remedies may be invoked where an investigation reveals "that the victim or other children at the institution is in imminent danger due to the continued contact between the alleged perpetrator and a child at the institution" (Colo. Rev. Stat. Sec. 19-3-308 [4] [c]).

A publicly employed teacher who is suspended for alleged child abuse is entitled to due process rights provided by Colorado's public employment laws as well as due process rights provided in either individual or group contractual agreements (Colo. Rev. Stat. Sec. 19-3-308 [4] [c]).

Several states have provisions in their reporting statutes that detail the conditions under which mandatory reporters, employed by school districts, have a duty to report suspected child abuse. California and Idaho require reports from school employees who discover abuse or neglect "within the scope of employment." New York joins with California and Idaho in requiring school employees to report child abuse or neglect discovered "within their professional or official capacity (N.Y. Soc. Serv. Law Sec. 413[1])." New York requires that the report be based on the reporter's "personal knowledge, facts, conditions or circumstances (N.Y. Soc. Serv. Law Sec. 413[1])," whereas California and Colorado require the reporter to have knowledge of or to have observed abuse before a report is made. Idaho limits this requirement simply to an observation of abuse. South Dakota is the only state that mandates school districts to have a written policy on reporting child abuse.

## Retaliation for Reporting Child Abuse or Neglect

Only six state reporting statutes contain a provision prohibiting employers from retaliating against mandatory reporters for making a report (see Appendix 10-B). Reporting statutes in Colorado, Florida, and Illinois specifically prohibit an employer from terminating a mandatory reporter for filing a report. Four states contain provisions expressly prohibiting an employer from retaliating against a mandatory reporter [90]. The Minnesota statute presumes that any adverse action against an individual within 90 days of a report of suspected abuse or neglect is retaliatory. However, this presumption is rebuttable (Minn. Stat. Ann., Sec. 626.557 subd. 17[c]). A facility or person found to have retaliated against a person for filing a report will be held liable for actual damages and a penalty of up to $10,000 (Minn. Stat. Ann., Sec. 626.557 subd. 17[b]). Two statutes simply prohibit discrimination against a reporter [91].

### States Affected

90. FL IL MA MN
91. ME MA

## Appendix 10-A: School Employees

- Harm caused by: AK CO FL

1. Mandatory reporter on school staff reports information to superintendent: CT
2. Certification revocation on conviction: CT
- Duties: AK CA
   1. District shall have a written policy on reporting: SD
   2. Knowledge of or observes abuse: CA CO
   3. Observes abuse: ID
   4. Reason to believe: FL ID
   5. Reasonable cause to suspect: CT
   6. School principal, superintendent, or delegate who knowingly and intentionally fails to report: SD
   7. States from personal knowledge, facts, conditions, or circumstances: NY
   8. Within scope of employment: CA ID
   9. Within professional capacity: CA ID NY

### Appendix 10-B: Termination of Employment

1. Cannot terminate reporter for reporting: CO FL IL
2. Employer cannot retaliate against mandatory reporter: FL IL MA MN
3. Employer adverse action is rebuttable presumption: MN
4. Employer who retaliates is liable for actual damages: MN
5. No discrimination against reporter: ME MA

# Summary of Findings and Actions:
# When Are They Available?

After the department completes its investigation of suspected child abuse or neglect, a physician or the head of an institution or school in Nebraska may, on request, receive a summary of the department's findings regarding a specific report of child abuse as well as a summary of actions the department has taken in response to the report. Thus far, only Nebraska's reporting statute contains such a provision (see Appendix 11-A).

### Appendix 11-A: Summary of Findings and Actions

1. Physician or head of institution/school: NB
2. Request, On: NB

# Conclusions and
# Recommendations

The language of the law often appears, on its face, to be clear and precise, but in reality the language of the law is very complex and frequently eludes precise parameters. Therefore, educators must exercise care in reading statutory requirements in order to avoid legal problems. Despite the complexity of some statutory language, educators need to familiarize themselves with their state child abuse reporting requirements ranging from who is considered a mandatory reporter to what information must be reported, to whom, and within what time frame. These four categories of information are essential to establishing a legitimate case against an individual who has abused a child and, ultimately, to protecting a victim of abuse from further harm. Educators need to take more responsibility for their own legal education, either through training in school law generally or by familiarizing themselves with statutory requirements available to all school districts through state education departments or local law libraries and courthouses.

In addition, although most reporting statutes do not specifically define components of a child abuse training program, educators could develop a comprehensive training program within the district and require all school employees who have contact with children to attend, at a minimum, an initial training session. Follow-up training, at intervals of two or more years, would enable all educators to be informed of changes in their states' child abuse reporting statutes. Interestingly, in doing this research, I discovered that state legislators are constantly tinkering with their reporting statutes. The requirement of one training session for educators simply is insufficient to ensure that all school district employees will remain current after the initial training.

Finally, school employees cannot continue to defer to the district's attorney. In many instances, errors are made at the outset, because of ignorance of the law, that lead to additional errors subsequently. Unfortunately, most school attorneys are not consulted before any action is taken. The result, in districts where school employees are not knowledgeable in the specifics of the law, is exposure to civil and possibly criminal liability in the area of child abuse reporting. Through inservice training or additional training and coursework, educators can become more confident in the steps they take to comply with the language of the law.

# Resources

## List of State Abbreviations

| | | | |
|---|---|---|---|
| Alabama | AL | Minnesota | MN |
| Alaska | AK | Mississippi | MS |
| Arizona | AZ | Missouri | MO |
| Arkansas | AR | Montana | MT |
| California | CA | Nebraska | NB |
| Colorado | CO | Nevada | NV |
| Connecticut | CT | New Hampshire | NH |
| Delaware | DE | New Jersey | NJ |
| District of Columbia | DC | New Mexico | NM |
| Florida | FL | New York | NY |
| Georgia | GA | North Carolina | NC |
| Hawaii | HI | North Dakota | ND |
| Idaho | ID | Ohio | OH |
| Illinois | IL | Oklahoma | OK |
| Indiana | IN | Oregon | OR |
| Iowa | IA | Pennsylvania | PA |
| Kansas | KS | Rhode Island | RI |
| Kentucky | KY | South Carolina | SC |
| Louisiana | LA | South Dakota | SD |
| Maine | ME | Tennessee | TN |
| Maryland | MD | Texas | TX |
| Massachusetts | MA | Utah | UT |
| Michigan | MI | Vermont | VT |

| | | | |
|---|---|---|---|
| Virginia | VA | Wisconsin | WI |
| Washington | WA | Wyoming | WY |
| West Virginia | WV | | |

## Table of Statutes

1. Child Abuse Prevention and Treatment Act, 42 U.S.C., sec. 5101
2. 42 USCS sec. 1983
3. Ala. Code, sec. 26-15-1 et. seq. (Michie 1986 & Supp. 1992)
4. Alaska Stat., sec. 47.17.010 et. seq. (1990)
5. Ariz. Rev. Stat. Ann., sec. 13-3620 et. seq. (1989 & Supp. 1991)
6. Ark. Stat. Ann., sec. 12-12-501 et. seq. (1987 & Supp. 1992)
7. Cal. Penal Code, sec. 11165 et. seq. (West 1991 & Supp. 1992)
8. Colo. Rev. Stat., sec. 19-3-301 et. seq. (1987 & Supp. 1991)
9. Conn. Gen. Stat. Ann., sec. 17-38a et. seq. (West 1986 & Supp. 1992)
10. Del. Code Ann. tit. 16, sec. 901 et. seq. (1983 & Supp. 1990)
11. Fla. Stat. Ann., sec. 415.501 et. seq. (West 1985 & Supp. 1992)
12. Ga. Code Ann., sec. 19-7-5 (1991)
13. Haw. Rev. Stat., sec. 350-1 et. seq. (1985 & Supp. 1991)
14. Idaho Code, sec. 16-1601 et. seq. (1979 & Supp. 1992)
15. Ill. Ann. Stat., ch. 23, para. 2051 et. seq. (Smith-Hurd 1975 & Supp. 1992)
16. Ind. Code Ann., sec. 31-6-11-1 et. seq. (West 1987 & Supp. Burns 1992)
17. Iowa Code Ann., sec. 235A.1 et. seq. (West 1984 & Supp. 1992)
18. Kan. Crim. Code Ann. sec., 21-3609 (Vernon 1971 & Supp. 1992)
19. Ky. Rev. Stat. Ann., sec. 620.010 et. seq. (Michie 1990 & Supp. 1992)
20. La. Rev. Stat. Ann., sec. 403 et. seq. (West 1986 & Supp. 1992)
21. Me. Rev. Stat. Ann. tit. 22, sec. 4001 et. seq. (1992)
22. Md. Family Law Code Ann., sec. 5-701 et. seq. (1991)
23. Mass. Ann. Law ch 199, sec. 51A et. seq. (Law Co-op 1975) Mass. Gen. Laws Ann. ch. 119, sec. 51A (West Supp. 1992)
24. Mich. Comp. Laws Ann., sec. 722.621 et. seq. (West 1991 & Supp. 1991)
25. Minn. Stat. Ann., sec. 626.556 et. seq. (West 1992 & Supp. 1992)
26. Miss. Code Ann., sec. 43-23-1 et. seq. (1981 & Supp. 1992)

27. Mo. Stat. Ann., sec. 210.110 et. seq. (Vernon 1983 & Supp. 1992)
28. Mont. Code Ann., sec. 41-3-101 (1991 & Supp. 1992)
29. Neb. Rev. Stat., sec. 28-707 et. seq. (1989 & Supp. 1991)
30. Nev. Rev. Stat. Ann., sec. 432B.010 (Michie 1991)
31. N.H. Rev. Stat. Ann., sec. 169-c:1 et. seq. (1990 & Supp. 1991)
32. N.J. Stat. Ann., sec. 9:6-1 et. seq. (West 1976 & Supp. 1992)
33. N.M. Stat. Ann., sec. 32-1-1 et. seq. (1989 & Supp. 1992)
34. N.Y. Soc. Sev., sec. 411, 413, 419 (Consol. 1984 & Supp. 1992)
35. N.C. Gen. Stat., sec. 7A-536 (1989 & Supp. 1991), sec. 115C-400 et. seq. (1991 Supp.)
36. N.D. Cent. Code, sec. 50-25.1-01 (1989 & supp. 1991)
37. Ohio Rev. Code Ann., sec. 2151.42 1 et. seq. (Anderson 1990 & Supp. 1992)
38. Okla. Stat. Ann. tit. 21, sec. 843 et. seq. (West 1983 & Supp. 1992)
39. Or. Rev. Stat., sec. 418.740 (1991)
40. Pa. Cons. Stat. Ann., secs. 6115, 6301 (Purdon 1991)
41. R.I. Gen. Laws, sec. 40-11-1 et. seq. (Michie 1990 & Supp. 1991)
42. S.C. Code Ann., sec. 20-7-480 (Lawyers Cooperative Services 1985 & Supp. 1992)
43. S.D. Codified Laws Ann., sec. 26-8A-1 (Michie 1992 & Supp. 1992)
44. Tenn. Code Ann., sec. 37-1-401 (Michie 1991)
45. Tex. Fam. Code Ann., sec. 34.012 et. seq. (Vernon 1986 & Supp. 1992)
46. Utah Code Ann., sec. 62A-4-401 et. seq.; 62A-4-502 (Michie 1991 & Supp. 1992)
47. Vt. Stat. Ann. tit. 33, sec. 4911 et. seq. (1991 & Supp. 1991). Vt. Stat. Ann. tit. 13, sec. 1351 et. seq. (1974)
48. Va. Code Ann., sec. 63.1-248.1 et. seq. (Michie 1991 & Supp. 1992)
49. Wash. Rev. Code Ann., sec. 26.44.010 et. seq. (West 1986 & Supp. 1992)
50. W. Va. Code Ann., sec. 49-6A-1 et. seq. (Michie 1992 & Supp. 1992)
51. Wis. Stat., sec. 48.981 (1990 & supp. 1991-1992), 1991 Wis. Act. 160; 1991 Wis. Act 263 (Lexis 1992)
52. Wyo. Stat., sec. 14-3-201 et. seq. (Michie 1986 & Supp. 1992)
53. D.C. Code Ann., sec. 2-1351 et. seq. (Michie 1988 & Supp. 1992)

## Table of Cases

- Crowder v. Lash, 687 F.2d 996, 1006 (7th Cir. 1982)
- Davis v. Durham City Schools, 91 N.C. App. 520 (N.C. 1988)
- Draper v. United States, 358 U.S. 307 (1959)
- Harlow v. Fitzgerald, 457 U.S. 800, 102 S.Ct. 2727 at 2738-39 (1982)
- Kempster v. Child Protective Services of Department of Social Services, 515 N.Y.S.2d 807 (N.Y. App. Div. A.D.2 Dept., 1987)
- Ker v. California, 374 U.S. 23 (1963)
- Lehman v. Stephens, 148 Ill. App.3d 538 (Ill. App. Ct. 1986)
- Mattingly v. Casey, 24 Mass. App. Ct. 452, 509 N.E.2d 1220 (Mass. App. Ct. 1987)
- McDonald v. State, 71 Or. App. 751, 694 P.2d 569 (Or. App. 1985)
- Miller v. Beck, 440 N.Y.S.2d 691, 82 A.D.2d 912 (N.Y. App. Div. 1981)
- New Jersey v. T.L.O., 469 U.S. 325 (1985)
- Roman v. Appleby, 558 F.Supp. 449, 459 (E.D. Pa, 1983)
- Rubinstein v. Baron, 219 N.J. Super. 129, 529 A.2d 1061 (N.J. Super. L. 1987)
- Terry v. Ohio, 392 U.S. 1 (1968)
- Thomas v. Beth Israel Hospital, Inc., 710 F.Supp. 935 (S.D.N.Y. 1989)
- Thomas v. Chadwick, 224 Cal. App.3d 813 (Cal. 1990)
- Wood v. Strickland, 420 U.S. 308, 322, 95 S.Ct. 992, 1000 (1975)

## References

Annotation, Professional liability for failing to report child abuse. 38 A. Jr. Trials 22 (West 1989).

Besharov, Douglas J. (1986). Child abuse and neglect: Liability for failing to report. 22 Trial 67.